Survival Guide

D1572464

SALT LAKE CITY · UTAH

Bagley's Utah Survival Guide
Copyright 2008
Pat Bagley

Photos courtesy of
The Salt Lake Tribune
Printed in the United States

Editor: Dan F. Thomas

First Edition

9 8 7 6 5 4 3 2 1

ISBN 978-0-9801406-0-6

White Horse Books 1347 S. Glenmare St.
Salt Lake City, UT 84105   (801) 556-4615
www.utahwhitehorsebooks.com

Survival Guide

by
Pat Bagley

INTRODUCTION

Utah lies in the heart of the Intermountain West, nestled between the soaring Sierra Nevadas to the west and the imposing Rockies to the east. Actually, it's the cleavage between the two.

The cleavage, in this case, is called the Great Basin. Like the name suggests, it is a great bowl. Runoff from the mountains flows inward to the Great Salt Lake, where evaporation leaves behind a briny, minerally sea the size of New Jersey.

The first person to step foot in the state did so about ten thousand years ago. His name was Ted.

Ted was impressed.

The Great Salt Lake is the remnant of an ancient and much larger, inland sea. At its largest, Lake Bonneville covered most of the state and was a thousand feet deep. Trout the size of German shepherds swam in waters that were visited by mammoths and sabre-toothed cats.

Utah covers 85,000 square miles, much of which is federally owned land—picturesque national parks, forests and bombing ranges. Two hundred years ago there was about one person per square mile—mainly Shoshone, Gosute, Paiute and Navajo. Today there are thirty people per square mile, a third of one of those people are Native American.

Utah is about 70% Mormon. It is the home and headquarters of the Church of Jesus Christ of Latter-day Saints, or LDS Church. Mormon pioneers fleeing persecution called the place Deseret (deh-zer-ET) and dreamt of a religious utopia symbolized by a beehive, signalling cooperation and industry.

Congress had different ideas. It named the place "Utah" after the Ute Indians who lived here. It ruled the territory remotely from Washington, D.C., and withheld statehood until the residents promised to behave and be good Americans.

Far from being a refuge of radical religionists—as originally intended—Utah today is probably the most American place in the world.

Think: apple pie (or in this case, green Jell-O™). Think: minivans full of kids unloading at a megaplex theatre in a strip mall. Think: gorgeous, multi-hued sunsets that could only be the result of serious pollution. This place is about as American as you can get.

Utah is also American in another essential way. It is messy. The Mormon influence is undeniable, but it is not the only influence.

At first they were called "gentiles." Catholics, Protestants, Orthodox, Buddhists, Muslims, Hindus, secular humanists, even Jews—anyone not of the predominant faith who came and put down stakes. Now they're simply "non-Mormons" who have a reputation for griping.

There are other demographic shifts, too. Spanish is now heard more than anytime since Dominguez and Escalante wandered up from Mexico (without papers) in 1776.

And there are Mormons of different faiths, ranging from fundamentalist to "barely there."

But still, Utah is like nowhere else. It still is, and will always be, the Beehive State.

WELCOME to the BEEHIVE

Resistance
is Futile

This book is for two populations: those who are new to Utah—unfamiliar with its customs, history, culture, but curious nonetheless.

And those already part of The Hive.

No matter how well you think you know the predictable rhythms of The Beehive State—the church-going, scrapbooking, buttoned-down, minivanned, lime-jelloed, Republicanned amalgam that is Utah—the saucy wench can still surprise you like a mixed metaphor.

We are the state that invented "alternative lifestyles," as in the HBO series "Big Love."

Utah is identified with religion. Utah is that metal thingy that hangs from the buckle of the Bible belt. So why does saying "I am from Utah" provoke such a strong reaction among some Americans? Especially among those who are, or should be, our fellow travelers? You might as well be saying, "Hi there! I am from the western affiliate of the Taliban. We have so much in common!"

This book is an attempt to explain and encompass something as broad and deep as the Pacific in 128 pages.

With illustrations.

WELCOME TO *Utah*

*A HOLY OWNED AND OPERATED SUBSIDIARY OF THE CHURCH OF JESUS CHRIST OF LATTER-DAY SAINTS

THE BEEHIVE STATE

The Beehive in Utah is ubiquitous. It was adopted as a symbol and a hairstyle by Mormon pioneers as a way to symbolically say, "Buzz off!"

Actually, the beehive allusion comes from Mormon scripture. *The Book of Mormon* says that *deseret* means "honeybee" in a lost language. Deseret, then, conjures up at least half the notion of a land flowing with milk and honey.

Today, bees and beehives are seen on the state flag, state letterhead, Highway Patrol cruisers, and countless key chains, pens and shot glasses.

UTAH STUFF

Some of which will be explained later.

HISTORY

Sanitized for Your Protection

Utah's history began on July 24, 1847.

That is the date Brigham Young gazed out on the Salt Lake Valley, stretched forth his arm and proclaimed, "This is the place."

With that, a troop of weary, but doughty, pioneer emigrants descended into the desolate valley, determined to break sod, build homes and make the desert blossom as a rose.

In no time at all, the valley was filled with strip malls, tract housing, industrial parks and open pit mines.

History was off and running.

Soon there would be Olympic Games, land speed records, Miss Americas, singing Osmonds, Jeopardy champions and Love Sacs.

"THIS IS THE PLACE" MONUMENT ←

Before then, nothing much of note happened.

PIONEER DAY

In Utah, the 24th of July is more of a big deal than the Fourth of July. The arrival of the Mormon pioneers is celebrated with parades, picnics, fireworks and naturally, a rodeo. However, both holidays *will* be celebrated on other days if either falls on a Sunday. All celebratory activities are moved to the previous Saturday, leading to the curious practice of celebrating the 4th on the 3rd, or the 24th on the 23rd.

The same goes for Halloween.

Had the Indians, who inhabited the area for thousands of years, been a little more organized, the illegal immigration debate might have taken on a whole new complexion.

"THIS IS WHERE YOU APPLY FOR YOUR GREEN CARD" MONUMENT

TAKE A NUMBER

BEFORE HISTORY

Before there was history, there was something called prehistory. Even Utah has one. In fact, given today's social/political climate, Utah is lucky enough to have *two* prehistories!

THE CREATIONIST STORY

Utah is richly endowed with fossils from a previous era. The remains of gigantic reptiles are so numerous in the Beehive State that it is difficult to turn around without tripping over the bones of a creature the size of a house. Six thousand years ago, these creatures rubbed a loving God the wrong way and were exterminated. They are called dinosaurs.

Before their untimely extinction, these big guys lived in the Garden of Eden with Adam and Eve, and every other kind of thing that has ever lived. Since death was unknown in The Garden, *tyrannosaurus rexes* only chewed on lowly mammalians and then released them. They did this in order to deliver lessons in proper etiquette. Dinosaurs were big on etiquette.*

Everyone ate salads, romped in ponds and vied to give Adam and Eve pony rides. (Ponies had an unfair advantage in this pastime as they were, well, ponies.)

Then everything went to hell-in-a-handbasket. Eve ate an apple.

Mammals, even then, were notorious for their nasty habits. The grabbing of one's crotch and wiggling, in a vaguely pornographic manner, at shocked passersby was a favorite lewd joke of the hirsute class. This drove dinosaurs into spitting hissyfits, who, with their short forearms, couldn't reach as far.

18

She wasn't supposed to eat this forbidden fruit. An angel appeared with a flaming sword and threatened Adam with Excruciating Death For All Mankind Throughout All Generations if he followed Eve's lead and ate of the fruit.

Eve told Adam he would be sleeping on the couch forever if he didn't. And so, death came into the world.

With Eden gone to seed, all the dinosaurs wandered over to Utah where they told stories of the good old days giving pony rides to Adam and Eve. Eventually someone got tired of the ten thousandth telling of how they were "Eve's favorite," and ate the storyteller.

Someone had just invented a new favorite pastime. This was in the early afternoon of May 13th, 2012 B.C. It was a Wednesday.

A week or two later, the dinosaurs were killed in Noah's Flood. But they would have the last laugh. While drowning, they cleverly arranged themselves in discreet, geologic layers. Geologists in the future would be taken in by this practical joke and come up with something called "Evolution."

Adam & Eve riding "Trigger."

EVOLUTION

Given inconceivable spans of time with inconceivably numerous genetic mutations to fiddle with, organisms evolved defenses and counterdefenses which led to their successful adaptation or eventual extinction.

By the time people arrived, Utah had seen a hundred million generations grow fins, drag themselves onto mud flats and express themselves in an astonishing display of teeth and horns and claws and size and texture and color.

Allosaurus is the state Fossil

Utah was a hot house nursery for some of nature's more popular creations.

The really cool dinosaurs all called Utah home.

The ancestor of today's cats and dogs came from here, not to mention, camels and horses.

Bones of mammoths are found all over the state, including Sandy, Salt Lake and Park City.

UTAHRAPTOR

Found near Moab, this beast was 18 feet long, weighed a ton, and had a 16-inch sickle-shaped claw used to disembowel its prey.

One Hour = A Million Years

If one hour equals a million years, then . . .

Dinosaurs arrived in Utah 10 days ago.

Dinosaurs disappeared less than 3 days ago.

Modern humans evolved in Africa 12 minutes ago.

People, hunting mammoth and big game, arrived in Utah 1 minute ago.

Mormon pioneers settled Utah half a second ago.

Utahraptor lived 100 million years ago.

PIONEERS

Fleeing From
The Man

THE TREK WEST

Arriving by wagon and handcart, the suffering of the early Mormon pioneers can only be imagined.

BULLETIN OF THE PLAINS

Pioneers left news scribbled on bleached ox and buffalo skulls for those that would come later. Usually these noted miles travelled and the date.

Serious strains, however, were put on the buffalo population when personal ads started appearing on the trail.

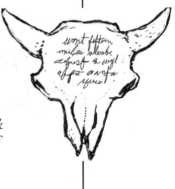

SWM, 23, fleeing mobs & persecution. Seeking SWF 18-25. Must be good with foot rubs.

No sooner had the Mormon pioneers settled down in their new home than they experienced their first miracle.

Crickets.

Billions of them. They were so ugly that the pioneers said they looked like a cross between a spider and a buffalo. Besides being ugly, they were voracious. They loved eating pioneer crops.

Commonly known as the "Mormon Cricket," (anabrus simplex) is not a cricket at all. It is really a species of grasshopper.

The pioneers were so moved at this first miracle that they demanded a second.

God sent flocks of dinosaurs* to eat the crickets. There is just no satisfying some people.

MIRACLE OF THE GULLS

The arrival of the cricket-eating gulls came just in time to rescue pioneer crops. The bird was cheered, celebrated and eventually made the state fowl of Utah. The fact that it is the California Seagull is less puzzling if you know that the state tree of Utah is the Colorado Blue Spruce.

It is generally accepted among paleontologists that dinosaurs didn't completely die out 65 million years ago. Birds are recognized as a surviving branch.

CRICKETS A LA CARTE

Those pioneers not interested in slow starvation took their cue from the indigenous population. Drawing on ten thousand years of experience, the Indians not only saw the cricket infestation as a God-given bonanza of nutritious protein, but a yummy treat, too.

"Cricket Poppers" are great with *lots* of salt.

DIDJA KNOW...

During the recent cricket infestation of 2003, snowplows were brought out to clear the roads of billions of tiny cricket corpses.

"HOW DO YOU KNOW THEY'RE MORMON CRICKETS?"

OLD TESTAMENT KIND OF FOLKS

Mormon pioneers saw themselves as literal descendants of the House of Israel. It was only natural for them to draw parallels between their experience and that of the ancient Hebrews.

JEWS	MORMONS
Jews are from the House of Israel.	*Mormons claim to be from the House of Israel by way of Scandanavia.*
Led by a prophet (Moses) through the wilderness (Sanai) to a promised land (Canaan).	*Led by a prophet (Brigham Young) through the wilderness (Nebraska) to a promised land (Utah).*
Land of promise has a freshwater lake (Galilee) which feeds into a salt lake (The Dead Sea) by way of the River Jordan.	*Land of promise has a freshwater lake (Utah Lake) which feeds into a salt lake (The Great Salt Lake) by way of the Jordan River.*
Everyone who is not one of them is a "Gentile."	*Everyone who is not one of them is a "Gentile."*

Early ambitions to establish a Mormon empire, presided over by a Priest-King, never really got past the talking stage.

POLYGAMY

wife 1.

wife 2.

wife 3.

wife 4.

wife 5.

wife 6.

wives 7-28.

Latter-day Lust

MORMON POLYGAMY

The first thing to know about polygamy is that it was a huge pain in the ass.

Mormons like to be liked and nobody liked polygamy.

They were ridiculed and chased half way across the continent to a desert because of it. They were invaded by the United States Army in 1857* because of it. Then they were tossed in the pokey for it, all through the 1870s and 1880s.

When, in 1890, LDS Church President Wilford Woodruff threw in the towel on the practice, most Mormons breathed a huge sigh of relief.

Ask any Mormon today and you'll be told that polygamy was a "test" from God. God has since moved onto a test involving strict monogamy, minivans and lots of kids.

"YES, MORMONS USED TO PRACTICE POLYGAMY — PROOF OF ITS DIVINE ORIGIN IS THAT WE DIDN'T ENJOY IT FOR A SINGLE SECOND."

*Called "Buchanan's Blunder," the president sent pretty much the whole U.S. Army to liberate Utahns from a cruel dictator and impose democracy "throughout the broader Intermountain West." It proved to be a big waste of time and money.

Many people coming to visit the "Mormon State" for the first time often have peculiar notions about what they'll find.

POLYGAMY'S ROOTS

In 1844, the church's founder, Joseph Smith, was assassinated by a hard-drinking, tobacco-chewing mob of Illinoians because he was so hardworking, thrifty, practical and God-fearing.

That and the fact that he "married" thirty-two women, which was stoutly denied.

So the Mormons packed up grandma and the ~~wives~~ wife and fled to the Utah Territory, where they could peacefully worship the wrathful God of the Old Testament, who had a different understanding of polygamy.

REPUBLICANS RUIN EVERYTHING

In 1856, the newly invented Republican Party condemned polygamy as one of the "twin evils of barbarism." The other twin was slavery.*

This staunch stand against Mormons and Southerners eventually led to the Civil War and later, the Edmunds-Tucker Act, which put the hammer down on polygamy.

After mopping up the South, the ascendant Republican Party turned its attention to Utah and the Mormons.

The tortured relationship between the early Republican Party and polygamist Utah was finally resolved in the early 20th century, when, after suffering the first documented case of mass

*Originally introduced at the Republican convention as the "Quadruplet Evils of Barbarism: Slavery, Polygamy, non-Prescription Opium and The Wearing of Funny Hats," it was agreed by party bosses in smoke-filled back rooms to streamline the motion and resubmit it to the assembly.

"Stockholm Syndrome," Mormons became enthusiastic members of the Party of Their Longtime Persecutors.* From fleeing The Man to being The Man—all in one generation.

Early church leaders imprisoned for practicing polygamy. Despite their imposing fashion sense, time in The Big House failed to earn them street cred in the hip hop community.

POLYGAMY TODAY

Not everyone gave up on polygamy. Splinter groups spread throughout the West to continue "spiritual wifery." Today there are an estimated 50,000 polygamists in Utah.

Polygamists claim to be merely practicing the freedom of religion granted in the Constitution for middle-aged men to marry fourteen-year-old girls.

On a personal note, I will never understand Utah's Mormons who are happy to carry water into the present day for people who hate them. Evangelicals, an important block of the Republican base, consider Mormons heretics and their religion a cult.

MARK TWAIN

on

POLYGAMY

from
Roughing It

"Our stay in Salt Lake City amounted to only two days, and therefore we had no time to make the customary inquisition into the workings of polygamy and get the usual statistics and deductions preparatory to calling the attention of the nation at large once more to the matter. I had the will to do it. With the gushing self-

> *I was feverish to plunge in headlong and achieve a great reform here — until I saw the Mormon women . . .*

sufficiency of youth I was feverish to plunge in head-long and achieve a great reform here—until I saw the Mormon women. Then I was touched. My heart was wiser than my head. It warmed toward these poor, ungainly and pathetically "homely" creatures, and as I turned to hide the generous moisture in my eyes, I said, "No — the man that marries one of them has done an act of Christian charity which entitles him to the applause of mankind, not their harsh censure — and the man that marries sixty of them has done a deed of open handed generosity so sublime that the nations should stand uncovered in his presence and worship in silence."

34

RELIGION

The Elephant in
the Room

THE MORMON QUESTION

Even if you're only in Utah for a short time, you are still going to want to get your head around this whole Mormon thing.

It is no easy task, because Mormonism is so big. Big like an elephant. In fact, it's like that fable of the blind men feeling different parts of an elephant and getting entirely the wrong picture. One "sees" a snake. Another, a pillar.

You need to step back and see the whole elephant. Then it becomes strikingly clear.

Mormons are Republicans.

THE MORMON ANSWER

Mormons comprise 70% of Utah's population, 90% of the state legislature and 100% of the moral tenor.

Mormons are Utah—get over it. Life isn't fair.

So now that you're here, what is a Mormon? A Mormon is a member of The Church of Jesus Christ of Latter-day Saints. A member of The Church of Jesus Christ of Latter-day Saints is a kind of Christian. The kind who thinks that a mere ten commandments is for wussies.

MORMON COMMANDMENTS

Mormons don't drink alcohol, coffee or tea (the uber-devout shun caffeinated drinks in all their hellish forms: Coke, Diet Coke, Diet Lime Coke, Vanilla Coke, Diet Vanilla Cherry Coke, etc. etc....), smoke, or have extramarital sex. They have large families (Utah rivals many third world countries in its rate of fertility. Only recently has Bangladesh squeeked ahead in the baby derby), drive minivans, squirrel stocks of food away for a rainy day or the end of the world, tithe ten percent, are eternally engaged in church work and still find the time and energy to appear pathologically happy to the neighbors.

Officially, Mormons don't like to be called Mormons.

The Church of Jesus Christ of Latter-day Saints press office would like The Mormon Church to be referred to in print and electronic media as The Church of Jesus Christ of Latter-day Saints. Members of the church are Members of the Church of Jesus Christ of Latter-day

Saints and should be referred to as such.

"LDS" will do in a pinch.

The Mormons have been engaged in a struggle, ongoing since 1890, to convince Christian America that it is not some weird cult. That it does, in fact, worship the same Jesus Christ as the rest of the nation.

In the 1980s, the church even added the subtitle, "Another Testament of Jesus Christ," to *The Book of Mormon.* So it's more like, *The Gospel: The Director's Cut*, with deleted scenes and director's commentary.

THE BOOK OF MORMON

The Book of Mormon is a take-it-or-leave-it proposition. You either have a burning spiritual conviction that in 1824, an eighteen-year-old in upstate New York was instructed by an angel to recover and translate an ancient history, written on gold plates, that tells of Hebrews fleeing Jerusalem before it was sacked by the Assyrians in 600 B.C., and sailing to America, where Jesus came to teach their descendants the Gospel following His crucifixion....

Or you don't.

The Church Office Building (COB) in downtown Salt Lake City is the bureau-cratic headquarters of the LDS Church. It looks nothing like a penis.

DIDJA KNOW...

The elevation of the top of the COB is just a little higher than the top of the state capitol building?

CHURCH FINANCES

Since the Church of Jesus Christ of Latter-day Saints is not obligated to reveal its financial statements to the public, estimates of its wealth by interested observers range from "fiscally healthy" to "richer than God."

MORMON TEMPLES ARE RESTRICTED TO MEMBERS IN GOOD STANDING. SWORN TO STRICT SECRECY MORMONS WILL NEVER REVEAL WHAT TRANSPIRES BEHIND THOSE TWELVE-FOOT-THICK GRANITE WALLS — SO JUST FORGET EVEN TRYING TO GET ONE TO TELL YOU ABOUT the NUBILE YOUNG VIRGINS and the VELVET PLAYMATE ROOM.

GENERAL AUTHORITIES

The top tier of leaders of the Church of Jesus Christ of Latter-day Saints are commonly referred to as "General Authorities." This is because they are authorities on generally everything.

They are also, generally, old. And white. And male.

The Hierarchical Structure of the Church of Jesus Christ of Latter-day Saints

← PRESIDENT

← FIRST PRESIDENCY

← COUNCIL of the TWELVE

← SEVENTY

← STAKE PRESIDENT

← BISHOP

← HEAD OF HOUSEHOLD

← LOVELY WIFE and MOTHER

FRUITFUL

Mormons are famously fecund. Likely the most fecund people in the United Sates. In fact, fecundity is encouraged in Mormon culture. Fecundedness is a hallmark of righteousness and a badge of honor.

There are any number of jokes told at the expense of Mormon fecundity.

For example, why do Mormon women stop having children at 39?

·Because 40 is just too many.

What is a minivan in Utah Valley with only four kids?

·A sure sign of impotence.

A small Mormon family.

DIDJA KNOW...

Children in Utah are denoted as a bunch (4-5), a crowd (6-8), a passel (9-10) and a full quiver (11 or more)?

SEX AND THE SAINTLY

Mormons are notoriously promiscuous in the many and varied expressions of their sexual self-control.

Mormons are not allowed to touch themselves, or anyone else, until married.

A local author once attempted a book called *Sex and the Single Mormon*. It was a flop. Who wants to spend $12.95 for two hundred blank pages?

Good Mormons are so disciplined that they are careful to avoid suggestive pictures of naked women, or even suggestions of suggestive pictures of naked women.

Warning!

Good Mormons will skip the next page, as it features gratuitous female nudity!

I said, "good Mormons."

MORMON THEOLOGY

The nub of Mormon theology is contained in four books —*The Bible, The Book of Mormon, The Pearl of Great Price, The Doctrine and Covenants.* One can prayerfully burrow through dense passages in unfamiliar English and eventually be rewarded with morsels of inspired truth.

Or you can buy the complete "Battlestar Galactica" DVD series (the original with Lorne Greene, not the new one with Edward James Olmos).

MORMONISM	BATTLESTAR GALACTICA
Identified with Twelve Tribes.	*Identified with Twelve Colonies.*
Political structure of a President and Quorum of the Twelve.	*Political structure of a President and Council of the Twelve.*
Center of the universe is a star called Kolob.	*Center of the universe is a star called Kobol.*
The enemy of mankind is Lucifer.	*Lucifer is a really nasty Cylon.*
Marriage is for "time and all eternity."	*Marriage is "not only for now, but for all eternity."*
"The glory of God is intelligence, or in other words, light and truth."	*"The glory of the universe is intelligence."*
God is an advanced man. "As man is, God once was; as God is, man may become."	*Space angels from the episode, "War of the Gods," explain: "As you are now, we once were. As we are now, you may become."*

When we return, more of... 'Mormons: Ordinary people just trying to become gods...'

Mormons are notoriously busy. Most of this busyness is coordinated through a rigorous schedule of meetings that are shoe-horned in between meetings meant to boost one's spiritual welfare.

On a typical Sunday there is a Relief Society meeting, a Priesthood meeting, a Sunday School meeting, a meeting for Primary and a Sacrament meeting. That's not counting the myriad of meetings of lay leaders to make sure all these meetings run smoothly.

During the week there is High Council, Mutual, Home Teaching, Visiting Teaching, Scouts and Family Home Evening. Scratch the whole day if it's a trip to the temple.

Exhaustion eats up whatever scrap of time might be left over for sin.

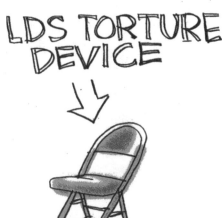

LDS TORTURE DEVICE

BLAME THE MORMONS

Besides giving us low rates of crime, tidy neighbor-hoods, not to mention children who are educated way beyond what you would expect from the lowest school funding in the nation, Mormons serve another function essential to the smooth running of a modern society.

Scapegoats.

Is your love life crummy? Is your job lousy? Can't find a good capuccino on Temple Square?

Blame the Mormons.

DIDJA KNOW...

> Utah has the lowest cancer rates in the nation?
> Blame the Mormons.

"YOU MORMONS ARE SO BIZARRE!"

JACK MORMON

A variety of Mormon who has given up strict adherence to Church commandments and rules. Easily identified because he is one of the few people in your neighborhood who is truly relaxed on The Day of Rest.

Also known as "retired Mormon," or "Mormon Emeritus."

OTHER RELIGIONS

Utah also has other religions.

GEOGRAPHY

There You Are

MAP DYSLEXIA

Millions suffer in silence the shame of not knowing which side Utah is jiggered on.

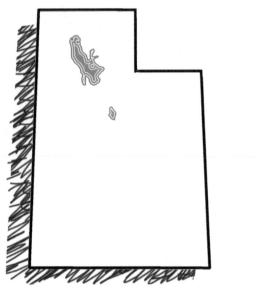

Can
You
Tell?

Out, Out, Damned Notch!

The drive by the conservative Sutherland Institute to invade Wyoming (or is it Idaho?) to "tidy things up," is gaining traction.

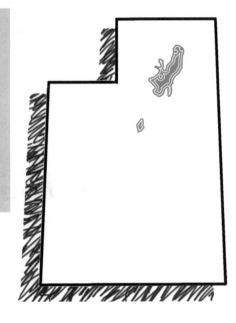

UTAH PLACE NAMES

This section will help you with the pronunciation and interpretation of certain unique names and designations one may encounter while travelling through the state.

La Verkin (la-VER·kuhn) A corruption from the Spanish "La Virgen." La Verkin is located on the Virgin River.

Hurricane (HER·kuhn) No kidding; two syllables. It is the town right next door to La Verkin.

Toquerville (TOE·ker·vil) A guaranteed favorite of stoners.

Tooele (Two·ill·UH) It's three syllables. Never say "Two-lee."

Manti (MAN·tie) Something featured in certain esoteric men's magazines.

Mantua (MAN·two·way) An act still illegal in Utah.

Monticello (Mon·tuh·SELL·oh) Not the way Jefferson would pronounce it, but he never made it out to Utah.

Peoa (pee·OH·uh) Oh!

Cache (cash) The "e" is very quiet.

Koosherem (coo·SHARE·um) It's just fun to say.

Hooper (HUH·per) You've probably got to go back to some backwater Hillbilly place in England to figure out where this came from.

Duchense (dew·SHANE) Surprisingly faithful to the original French.

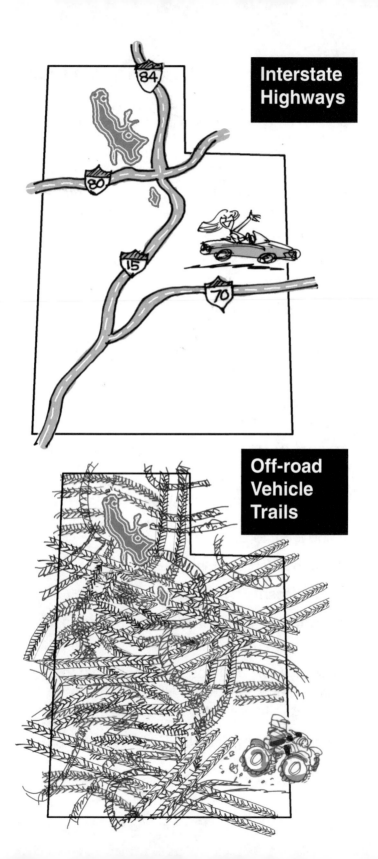

Interstate Highways

Off-road Vehicle Trails

Early in the George W. Bush administration it was discovered Utah had a lot of empty land. Land just sitting there looking pretty. Tons of it. As far as the eye could see in some instances.

And it was quiet. Too quiet.

Since scenery doesn't do anything for the GDP, the Bush people decided to put it to work. Soon all that land was gainfully employed as oil and gas fields, strip mines and fodder for saw mills.

Talks are still under way to turn our national parks, like Zion and Bryce, into private gated communities.

DIDJA KNOW...

One of the few man-made objects visible from space is a hole in Utah—the Kennecott open pit copper mine in the Oquirrh Mountains?

" SOMEDAY, SON, NONE OF THIS WILL BE YOURS..."

In 1968, 6,000 sheep suddenly dropped dead in Skull Valley. The Army never officially accepted responsibility for a nerve gas test gone awry, but paid off the sheepherders anyway.

Utah is home to 19 Superfund Sites, areas deemed so toxic that they require immediate attention. Nine of these are quaintly nestled in the heavily populated Salt Lake valley.

Energy Solutions, a Utah corporation, imports God knows how many tons of low level nuclear waste from all over the U.S. and God knows where else.

Utah is proud to host the largest bombing range in America.

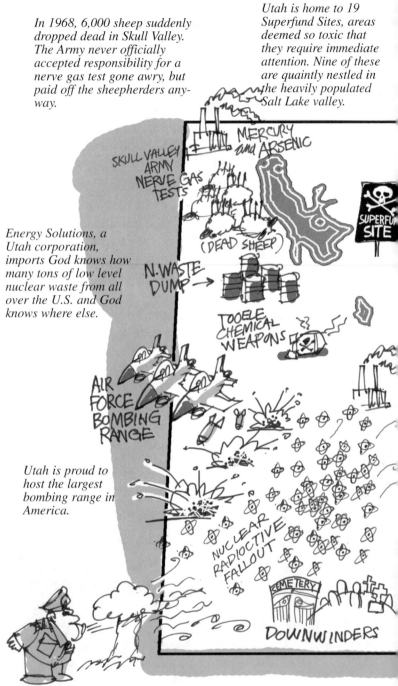

Boy, oh boy. Where to begin? Throughout the 50s and 60s the U.S. military tested nearly a thousand nuclear weapons in the Nevada desert. Radioactive fallout was blown east into Utah and was detected as far away as New York State. A spate of exotic cancers sprouted in Southern Utah. Those who died as a result of nuclear testing are called "Downwinders." By the way, John Wayne starred in several Westerns shot in Utah at the time. He died of stomach cancer in 1979.

I ☢ UTAH map

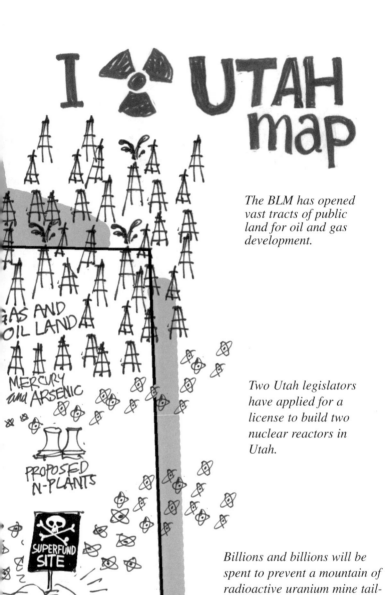

GAS AND OIL LAND

MERCURY and ARSENIC

PROPOSED N-PLANTS

SUPERFUND SITE

URANIUM TAILINGS

The BLM has opened vast tracts of public land for oil and gas development.

Two Utah legislators have applied for a license to build two nuclear reactors in Utah.

Billions and billions will be spent to prevent a mountain of radioactive uranium mine tailings from seeping into the Colorado River, which is only a stone's throw away.

DIDJA KNOW.

A government official involved with the nuclear testing in Nevada once said, "Oh, God, I hope we didn't kill John Wayne!"?

---

*The Bonneville Salt Flats,
where you can see the curva-
ture of the earth.*

UTAH METROPOLISES

DIDJA KNOW....

Levan (luh·VAN), the town in the dead center of the state, is "Navel" spelled backwards?

Moab — A perfectly good uranium mining town gone bust until discovered by outdoor enthusiasts. Biking, rafting, hiking, camping, rock-climbing, four-wheeling.

Ogden — A perfectly good railroad town gone bust. Still trying to decide what it wants to be next.

Park City — A perfectly good, shee-shee ski resort and home to the world famous Sundance Film Festival. Now known for hosting 2002 Winter Olympics venues, it was once a silver mining town gone bust.*

Provorem — Home of the BYU Cougars and the intellectual center of the world for crack-pot reactionary neo-Birch Society institutes and get-rich-quick pyramid enterprises. But there are some good Mexican restaurants.

Saint George — In Mormon theology, there is a place people go after death, but before heaven. It is called The Spirit World. Saint George is the place Mormons go before they go to the Spirit World. Its relatively mild climate makes it the Coco Beach for Mormons. They can play a round of golf in the morning and do a temple session in the afternoon.

Salt Lake City — Capital city and crossroads of the West, it hosted the 2002 Winter Olympics in, uh, 2002. The center of The LDS Church and the state's most liberal residents live cheek by jowl in apparent harmony.

My parents had the opportunity to buy miner's shacks on Main Street in 1959 for $200. They passed on it. Way to go, Mom and Dad!

DRINKING in UTAH

Fine Whines

TIPPLING TRIP TIPS

Relax.

If you are new to Utah and appreciate a fine red—
one featuring light, almost fruity preludes followed
by profoundly lugubrious shin-kicking afternotes—
with your food, but have heard stories about Utah,
take heart! Both are possible (food *and* drink, I
mean).

Some like to complain about the shame and indigni-
ty of getting a drink in Utah. The byzantine rules,
the nonsensical laws, the absence of public intoxi-
cation . . . .

Granted, there are procedures which attend the serving of a Cosmo or an Irish Car Bomb in the
Beehive. For instance, one cannot have two of said
drinks in front of oneself at the same moment in the
present space-time continuum.

One must also buy food or a club membership to be
served alcohol or the universe will collapse in on
itself.

Nevertheless, whether you are a wine snob or a beer
guzzler, with a little study you can happily find
whatever appeals to your particular taste.

DIDJA KNOW...

*The 60-75% markup that you
pay for alcohol in Utah goes to
educating schoolchildren?
Here's looking at you, kids!*

THE 3.2% SOLUTION

BEER WITH AN ALCOHOL CONTENT BELOW 3.2% MAY BE SOLD IN GROCERY STORES and MINI-MARTS

ALL OTHER STUFF →

MUST BE PURCHASED AT A SECRET, UNDISCLOSED LOCATION CALLED the STATE LIQUOR STORE

The Department of Alcohol Beverage Control (DABC) enforces the regulations and laws passed by legislators who don't believe in drinking and want to remind you at every opportunity what a filthy habit it is.

If it wasn't so lucrative,
they'd ban it outright.

Hint: Don't blame your server if Utah liquor laws appear cumbersome and awkward.

"HERE'S YOUR WINE LIST..."

THE LIQUOR STICKER

It's okay to bring your own wine to a restaurant, but it better have the DABC sticker, which indicates it was purchased at a state outlet.

Authorized restaurants authorized to serve alcohol will provide an authorized server to open it for you. Be prepared to pay for the privilege.

THE UTAH LIQUOR COMMISSION

The Department of Alcohol Beverage Control Liquor Commission is a representative cross section of the community's white, male, Mormon, teetotaling lawyer population.

BOOTLEGGING

Bootlegging is illegal in Utah.

Therefore it would be inappropriate for me to let you know that Evanston, Wyoming, is an hour and a half drive from Salt Lake.

You certainly wouldn't be interested in the fact that it is a good place to procure kegs of beer (real beer, not that weak 3.2 stuff) and fireworks.

You also probably don't care that Wendover, Nevada, is only two hours due west of Salt Lake and has gambling and liquor sold in grocery stores. The Fun Bus leaves every Friday night and is back by Saturday morning.

UTAH WHINE

The People — Light, fruity, innocent. Sweet with friendly hints of simpler days. Very drinkable, but can turn sour if not taken at face value.

The Politics — Very, very, very red. Big bodied, brassy, loud, stubborn without pretentions of subtlety. A real kick in the gut to those used to more than one note in their reds. Proudly proclaims its lack of refinement and depth. Best served with huge slabs of red meat.

The Land — Beautiful, ephemeral. Dry, complex, whiffs of haunting land-scapes climb to bracing, higher, piney notes. A thrilling discovery for those with a taste for the extreme, yet also speaks soothingly to one's inner search for the sublime.

Always memorable and intoxicating when drunk in.

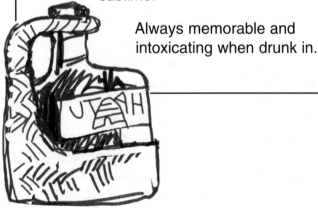

UTAH COCKTAIL

DIDJA KNOW....

In 1920, Utah enthusiastically supported the 18th Amendment, which ushered in prohibition?

JACK MORMON

One shot Jack Daniels

Half a jigger bitters

2 oz. Hawaiin Punch™

Ice

Serve with a sprig of rhubarb

DIDJA KNOW....

In 1933, Utah enthusiastically became the 36th, and deciding, state to vote for the 21st Amendment, which repealed the 18th Amendment?

FAVORITE SONS

SONS

. . . and daughters too!

Famous Utahns

Brigham Young

Born in New England in 1801, Brigham Young was an early convert to Mormonism and a devoted follower of Joseph Smith.

With Smith's assassination in 1844, several claimed to be his successor. Young, head of the Quorum of Twelve, won out over rivals by force of personality.

He never claimed to be much of a "revelator," but his sole revelation revealed an organizing genius. Brigham appointed captains and established a chain of command to bring wagon trains West. He used the same model to establish hundreds of well-ordered, tidy settlements in the Great Basin.

But he will forever be remembered for polygamy. He had around forty wives, eighty daughters and a hundred sons.

DIDJA KNOW...

Brigham Young is rumored to have run into a young man who looked vaguely familiar. He amiably inquired, "Young man, who's son are you?"

"Yours, sir!" the Young man replied.

MARTHA HUGHES CANNON

"MATTIE" CANNON WAS A DOCTOR, THE FOURTH WIFE OF ANGUS CANNON, AND A VOCAL PROPONENT OF WOMEN'S RIGHTS.

IN 1896 SHE RAN AS A DEMOCRAT AGAINST HER REPUBLICAN HUSBAND FOR THE UTAH SENATE —AND WON!

Reed Smoot

Reed Smoot, the Republican senator from Utah, was also a member of the Quorum of the Twelve Apostles of the Church of Jesus Christ of Latter-day Saints.

It took a while for his senatorial colleagues to warm up to him. Once they realized he was more interested in promoting business than religion, he became a respected member of the club.

He is credited with bringing Utah into the American political mainstream.

Napoleon Dynamite

I'm aware that Napoleon is an Idahoan. But did you know he was born in Utah County at Brigham Young University?

His parents were BYU students Jon Heder, who played the titular character, and Jared Hess, who wrote and directed the film.

Jon and Jared expanded their 2003 student film, *Peluca*, into the indie feature, which screened at the Sundance Film Festival and became an international smash hit.

Steve Young

Star BYU quarterback Steve Young had huge shoes to fill when he followed Joe Montana as the starting quarterback for the San Francisco 49ers. He proved himself by steering the team to a 1995 Superbowl championship.

His extended bachelorhood and residence in San Francisco set tongues wagging. His marriage to a former model deflated any number of fatuous fantasies.

And, yes, he is a direct descendant of Brigham Young.

Philo T. Farnsworth

It is said Philo first got the idea for television while picking beets. The radiating rows gave him an idea that would transform the world.

In 1927 he transmitted the first television picture. He spent the rest of his life in legal wrangling with RCA, which stole his idea.

The courts finally ruled in favor of Philo, who died shortly thereafter.

Miss Americas

Utah has produced two Miss Americas.

Colleen Kay Hutchins won the title in 1952. She went on to become the mother of Kiki Vandeweghe, an NBA player and a clutch shooter (though crummy on defense).

Sharlene Wells, daughter of an LDS general authority, was tapped to be Miss America in 1985. Her win came in the wake of Vanessa Williams's (Miss America 1984) scandalous Penthouse appearance.

Utah's Miss Wells seemed like a very, very safe bet.

Sharlene Wells broadcast for ESPN.

Donny and Marie

Donny and Marie took the pop world by storm, then conquered Country, becoming a fixture in Branson, MO. Their wholesome TV variety show was a national hit in the 70s.

The arrest of Paul Lynde, a frequent guest on the show, outside a gay bar in Salt Lake, may have had something to do with declining ratings.

However, friendship with Boy George and admission of postpartum depression have kept the duo current.

Orrin Porter Rockwell

Orrin Porter Rockwell once said he never killed a man "who didn't need killing."

Called "The Destroying Angel of Mormondom," he was a deputized Utah lawman who got his start as the bodyguard of Joseph Smith.

Legend has it Smith told him if he never cut his hair, blade or bullet would never hurt him.

Between bringing bad guys to justice and carrying out Brigham's instructions, he ran a tavern at Point of the Mountain, halfway between Salt Lake and Provo.

He died in his sleep.

Mitt Romney

Although born in Detroit, Romney became a native son after saving the scandal-ridden 2002 Salt Lake Olympics.

He used his success at turning the games around to launch a bid for governor of Massachusetts.

During the campaign, his moderate stance on abortion, gay rights, gun control and government-funded health care played well in this leftyist of states.

"I don't line up with the NRA"
—Old Mitt

Mitt Romney

In 2007 Mitt used his status as governor of a large state to launch a bid for President of the United States.

During the campaign, Mitt suddenly realized that he had *meant* to say that he was *against* abortion, gay rights, socialized medicine and *for* gun nuts.

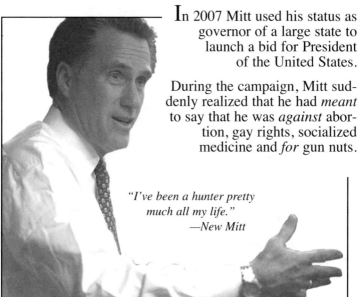

"I've been a hunter pretty much all my life."
—New Mitt

Ken Jennings

Ken Jennings, the gamer-phenom from Sandy, Utah, burst onto the gameworld scene like an affable, clean-cut Hurricane Katrina.

With ice-cold water flowing through his veins, he decimated his opponents with a storm surge of useless trivia. His clever strategy of clicking the buzzer first and coming up with the right answer, befuddled opponents and added to his growing pile of lucre.

Jeopardy has never seen the like.

He only lost out of boredom. Toying with mere mortal contestants lost its "zing." He has since satisfied a desire to conquer the literary world with a very readable book about trivia.

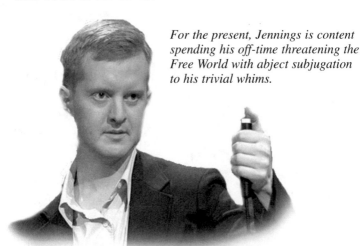

For the present, Jennings is content spending his off-time threatening the Free World with abject subjugation to his trivial whims.

Utah has more trivia per capita than any other state in the lower 48?

Notorious Utahns

Butch Cassidy

Warren Jeffs

The quality of Utah's "Most Wanted" went into steep decline following the 19th century.

George Leroy Parker—better known as the famous outlaw Butch Cassidy—was the son of a Mormon bishop. Along with the Sundance Kid, he was the heart and soul of the Hole-in-the-Rock Gang.

Born in 1866 in Beaver, Utah, young Butch fell in with a rough crowd, robbed trains, and was eventually killed in Bolivia.

One acquaintance remembered him as "the best cowboy I ever knew."

Warren Jeffs is the Prophet, Seer and Revelator of the polygamist Fundamentalist LDS Church, headquartered in Colorado City, Utah. He is currently serving time for ordering a fourteen-year-old girl to marry her older cousin.

Briefly achieving "Most Wanted" status on the FBI top ten list, he was convicted in 2007 for being an accomplice to rape.

Notorious Utahns (cont.)

Reed Smoot

Reed Smoot, Republican senator from Utah, claimed that banning James Joyce's *Ulysses* was his proudest achievement in Washington.

His cosponsorship of the Smoot-Hawley Act in 1929, a protectionist bill that was passed to save American industry from cheap imports, is credited with triggering the Great Depression.

Karl Rove

Rove spent his formative years in Salt Lake City, attending Olympus High School and verbally emasculating debate team opponents for fun.

He briefly attended the University of Utah before moving on to becoming a big fish in a Texas pond. His instinct to ruthlessly eviscerate political opponents at whatever cost to win drew the attention of Texas Republicans interested in bringing ethics back to government.

He became the moral compass for George W. Bush.

Roseanne Barr

Comedienne Rosanne Barr grew up Jewish in Salt Lake City. Some say she developed her acerbic wit as a way to cope with the unique culture here. Others say that she's just a jerk.

She once called Mormons, "Nazi Amish."

DIDJA KNOW...

In the 1880s, the federal government offered a $300 bounty for LDS Church President John Taylor, and $500 for George Q. Cannon, his counselor. They were on the lam for polygamy.

The lower reward for Taylor was a calculated insult.

RECREATION

Dude, Watch This!

THE OUTDOOR

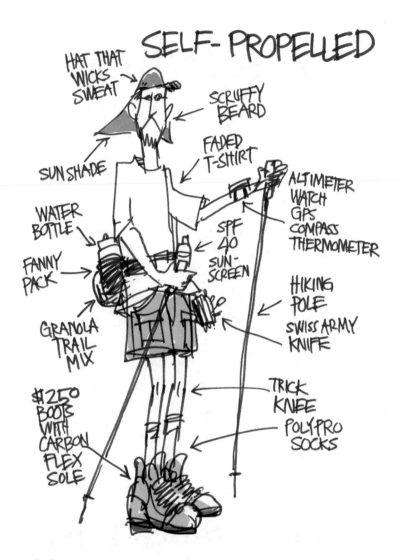

SELF-PROPELLED

HAT THAT WICKS SWEAT

SCRUFFY BEARD

FADED T-SHIRT

SUN SHADE

ALTIMETER
WATCH
GPS
COMPASS
THERMOMETER

WATER BOTTLE

SPF 40 SUN-SCREEN

FANNY PACK

HIKING POLE

SWISS ARMY KNIFE

GRANOLA TRAIL MIX

TRICK KNEE

$125⁰⁰ BOOTS WITH CARBON FLEX SOLE

POLYPRO SOCKS

More than any other state in the nation, Utah's riches lie in its natural beauty. It is worth going out for a look.

Some believe such looking should be done simply.

ENTHUSIAST

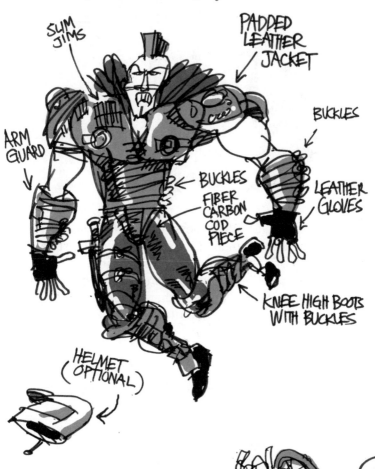

MOTORIZED

SLIM JIMS

PADDED LEATHER JACKET

BUCKLES

ARM GUARD

BUCKLES

FIBER CARBON COD PIECE

LEATHER GLOVES

KNEE HIGH BOOTS WITH BUCKLES

HELMET (OPTIONAL)

Others think it is better accompanied by the whine of torqued metal and roar of internal combustion.

OUR LAND

The Southern Utah Wilderness Association (SUWA) is one of many environmental organizations in the state. Its goal is to preserve habitat, protect endangered species, and raise the blood pressure of developers and Utah legislators (often one and the same) by way of lawsuits until their heads pop off.

Low-impact camping lets you get close to nature.

NATIONAL PARKS

Arches National Park — Home of the famous Delicate Arch, one of Utah's most recognizable icons.

Bryce Canyon National Park —Go find out what a *hoodoo* is.

Capitol Reef National Park — The only national park I know where you can pick fruit in the campgrounds.

Canyonlands — Utah's largest and most rugged national park.

Zion National Park — Utah's most popular tourist attraction—after Cabela's sporting goods in Lehi. (I'm not kidding).

People choose to experience Utah's outdoor wonders in various ways.

"DANG-WE FORGOT THE 'NATURE SOUNDS' CD."

The area around Moab, Utah, (which includes Arches National Park) is the world capital of mountain biking. Vast miles of wheel-friendly sandstone desert also attract legions of off-road vehicle enthusiasts.

MOAB

From Bombs to Bikes

Moab boomed in the 1950s, providing much of the uranium that gave America's 30,000 nuclear weapons their unique *oomph*! The town went bust when the government figured that having the ability to annihilate every living thing three times over was probably enough and stopped buying uranium.

From a tumbleweed ghost town, Moab bounced back to become a bustling tourist haven and the world's premier mountain biking venue.

BIKING

Biking is all about spandex.

If you don't look good in skin-tight, artificial fabric, then maybe you should stick to bowling.

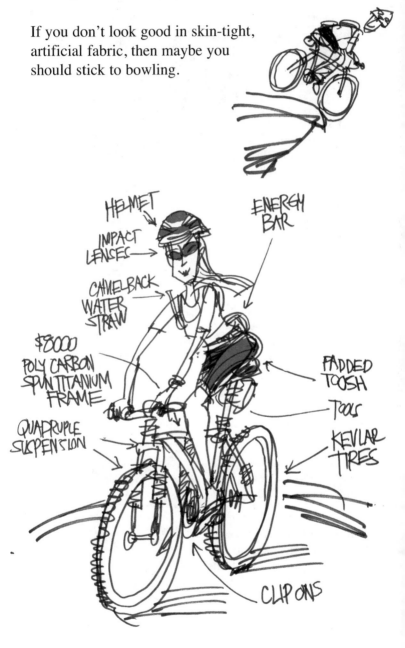

HELMET

IMPACT LENSES →

CAMELBACK WATER STRAW

$8000 POLY CARBON SPUN TITANIUM FRAME

QUADRUPLE SUSPENSION

ENERGY BAR

PADDED TOOSH

TOOLS

KEVLAR TIRES

CLIP ONS

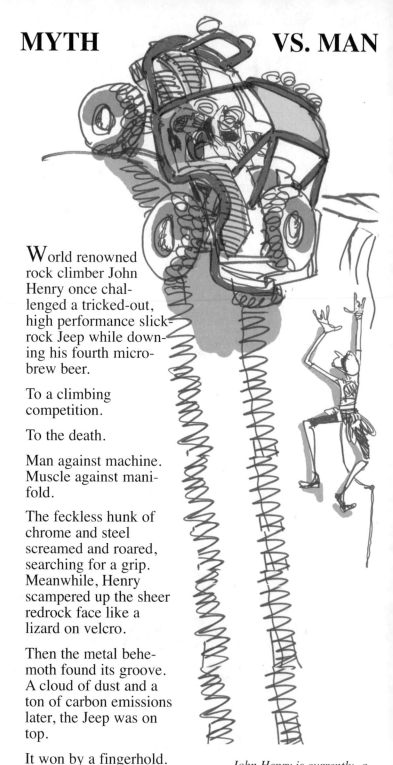

World renowned rock climber John Henry once challenged a tricked-out, high performance slickrock Jeep while downing his fourth microbrew beer.

To a climbing competition.

To the death.

Man against machine. Muscle against manifold.

The feckless hunk of chrome and steel screamed and roared, searching for a grip. Meanwhile, Henry scampered up the sheer redrock face like a lizard on velcro.

Then the metal behemoth found its groove. A cloud of dust and a ton of carbon emissions later, the Jeep was on top.

It won by a fingerhold.

John Henry is currently a barista at a Moab java joint.

HUNTING AND FISHING

SKILL and PATIENCE REWARD THE SERIOUS ANGLER.

WHIRLING SICKNESS

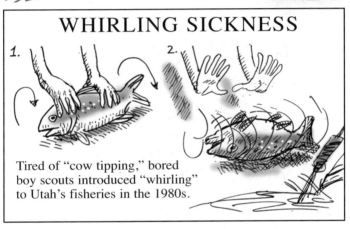

1.

2.

Tired of "cow tipping," bored boy scouts introduced "whirling" to Utah's fisheries in the 1980s.

The annual deer hunt (or "harvest") in late October has been going on for so long that only the most cunning and lethal mule deer have been left to breed.

SKIING
Going Downhill Fast

Skiing in Utah came of age when members of the Army's 10th Mountain Division, which trained here for winter combat, came back after WWII. Schussing down Utah's spectacular slopes was the most fun these GIs ever had.

But with a full-day ski pass currently close to $100, GIs can no longer afford it.

SUNDANCE

Once a local event to help struggling, independent filmmakers, the Sundance Film Festival was hijacked by the rich and powerful as another excuse to snort coke and party in scenic venues. Each January, the famous and beautiful descend on Park City. The Little People go to gawk at their betters.

Nobody goes for the movies anymore.

THIS IS FUN. →

SNOWBOARDING
Skiing's Bastard Child

Snowboarding was started as a way to introduce a new generation to the slopes. That, and to piss off skiers.

At first, few knew what to make of the monopods.

When it became clear that strapping one's feet to a single board was something akin to man-uevering Salem's punishment stocks at high speed down a mountain, many long-time skiers took up tennis.

Nonetheless, it is now a sanctioned Olympic sport which means it is here to stay. Along with synchronized swimming and curling.

DUDE! <u>SICK</u> FRONTSIDE FIVE-FORTY STALEFISH, DUDE !!!

DIDJA KNOW...

"Dude, I didn't see ya!"
is snowboarder for "Sorry?"

2002 OLYMPICS

After trying so hard for so many years to land the Olympics honestly, Salt Lake was finally awarded The Games when it wised up to how The Game was played.

You had to grease the skids.

For example, in previous years Salt Lake sent snowballs packed in styrofoam to African Olympic delegates. Nagano sent freezers full of snowballs—Japan won that year.

Like the good kid who is caught the first time pocketing a roll of lifesavers at the Piggly Wiggly, the Salt Lake Olympic Committee was fingered for bribing Olympic officials.

"But everybody else does it!" didn't go down well with Utahns whose money was being used to wine and dine Euro-trash sport officials.

"WHERE DO WE GET BRIBED?"

Finally, Utah gets some press that doesn't have to do with weird, nineteenth century religious practices.

Despite starting off on the wrong foot, the Salt Lake Olympic Games managed to pull itself together during the rest of the routine, finishing with an exquisite triple sow cow, double lutz combination—a very high degree of difficulty—to land a perfect score.

Yesss!

FLIP!

Olympic Savior

No matter how one views Mitt Romney's pandering to become president, you've got to give him credit for a bang-up job on the Olympics.

Heck, he even reportedly dropped the F-bomb when a traffic snarl threatened to gum up a venue.

POLITICS

Neocons Gone Wild!

The separation of church and state in Utah is about three blocks.

POLITICS IN THE BEEHIVE

Politics in Utah is a churchy-state kind of thing.

Ferreting out where one ends and the other begins can be a real brain-teaser. I've already mentioned that one of Utah's first U.S. senators, Reed Smoot, was also a member of the Quorum of the Twelve.

Even before statehood, the territorial legislature, under Governor Brigham Young, would adjourn one minute and convene the next as something called The Council of Fifty, a priesthood quorum charged with the political administration of The Kingdom of God.

In time, religious tenets merged with commercial interests to make modern Utah—it's a long story.

Separation of church and state in Utah is unthinkable. Not after they've been married—or at least been in bed together—for as many years as they have.

STANDING ON PRINCIPLE

Not that long ago a panel was commissioned to look into Utah liquor laws. The idea was to streamline embarrassingly obsolete and cumbersome rules governing the dispensing of wine and spirits.

The panel did its job and came up with sensible reforms. It only needed one legislator to endorse their recommendations to put it for a vote.

None would. Liquor is the "third rail" of Utah politics.

Having devoted so much time and effort, the commission showed its proposed reforms to The Church.

The Church saw no problem.

Word got back to the legislature before the commission did. The recommendations were enthusiastically cosponsored by every single state senator and enacted as law.

"SISTER FINCH, I'M TIRED OF ALL THESE STORIES IN THE MEDIA THAT SAY THE CHURCH CALLS ALL THE SHOTS IN UTAH —HAVE THE LEGISLATURE PASS A RESOLUTION DENYING IT!"

THE UTAH LEGISLATOR

WELL-FED NORDIC LOOK

CARRIES A CONCEALED WEAPON IN CASE A MEMBER of the PUBLIC GETS TOO CLOSE

NAVY BLUE SUIT

WHITE SHIRT

CALF LEATHER HOLSTER that MATCHES SCRIPTURE TOTE

HAS BETWEEN 7 and 12 KIDS (WHAT WITH WORK, CHURCH, PROJECTS, LEGISLATURE and TIME at JAZZ GAMES WITH LOBBYISTS, HE CAN ONLY OFFER an EDUCATED GUESS.)

IS PROUD NOT TO HAVE TAKEN PART IN EVOLUTION

REPUBLICANS RULE!

The Grand Old Party is the Official State Party of Utah. Nine out of ten public offices are held by Republicans.

Republicans call the shots in this enlightened, bucolic, well-armed, one-party state.

Do You Have What It Takes to Be a Moral Majority?

Utah legislators, always on the cutting edge of crazy, have a unique perspective on the whole universe.

DIDJA KNOW...

A prominent republican politician from southern Utah scoffed at the notion that radiation was dangerous. He wore a bollo tie clip made of uranium to prove it.

He died of throat cancer.

DIDJA KNOW...

Legislators in the 2004 session told each other that "B" and "C" nuclear waste was safe enough to brush one's teeth with?

THE GUN-LOVINGEST STATE IN THE WHOLE DERN SHOOTIN' MATCH

In 1996 the state legislature made toting a concealed weapon easy. So easy that it's almost mandatory.*

Fifty bucks, a driver's license, a two hour gun safety course and you're ready to sling iron like your favorite TV detective.

Churches, businesses and private residences must post notice if they object to guns on the premises.

Public schools and universities have no such luck. Miss Mapplethorp, your kid's kindergarten teacher, might very well be packing heat and you parents have no right to know.

VIRGIN →

*The southern Utah town of Virgin (population 400) passed ordinances that mandated ownership of a loaded firearm. Just down the highway, La Verkin (population 3,500) forbade the United Nations from operating within city limits.

DIDJA KNOW...

*The current head of the NRA said, "...we believe in absolutely, gun-free, zero-tolerance, totally safe schools. That means **no** guns in America's schools. Period."?*

DIDJA KNOW...

A gun in the home is way, way more likely to be used on oneself or a family member than on an intruder?

DIDJA KNOW...

8% of all permits are denied or revoked for crimes ranging from domestic violence and murder to "moral turpitude?"

DIDJA KNOW...

There are more licensed gun dealers than there are McDonald's restaurants?

DIDJA KNOW...

A well-armed society is a scared society?

DIDJA KNOW...

90,000 concealed weapons permits are on Utah's books—more than three times the number of all the armed terrorists in Hamas, Al Qaeda, Hezbollah and the Mahdi Army combined?

UTAH DEMOCRAT

THIS SHY, RETIRING CREATURE IS RARELY SEEN — SOME SAY IT IS A MYTH, AKIN TO "SNIPES" — though SITINGS HAVE BEEN REPORTED AT QUIET SALT LAKE BISTROS

Utah Democrats are a lonely lot.

It is joked that all the Democrats here can meet in a phone booth.

Lately, Democrats have made some inroads. Now they meet in a shipping container.

DEER-IN-THE-HEADLIGHTS LOOK

DIDJA KNOW...

Ezra Taft Benson, one-time president of the LDS Church, said that one could not be a good Mormon and a Democrat at the same time?

REPUBLICANS RULE!

A Utah Democrat is like a Chicago Cubs fan, only without the hope.

In 2000 and 2004, Utah gave George W. Bush his largest winning margin of any state. It was also the last state to give the colossally unpopular Bush administration negative ratings in the polls—in 2007.

The 2nd Congressional District traditionally elects a Democrat. But said Democrat must walk, talk and squawk like a Republican to retain his seat.

"WE HAD THE LAST ONE STUFFED"

DIDJA KNOW...

In 2006 the LDS Church said in an official statement that it was okay to be a Democrat?

FLORA and FAUNA

Natural Utah

THE BEAR LAKE MONSTER
Nessy's Sis?

Loch Ness in Scotland may lay claim to the popular imagination when it comes to aquatic beasties, but Utah has scientifically valid reasons to believe there may be a connection between Bear Lake and its Scottish sister-body-of-water.

Sitings of the Bear Lake Monster date to the 1860s.

THE HONEYBEE

Admired by the Mormon pioneers for its unstinting industry and ability to work until it dropped dead, the honeybee was adopted as the state insect in 1983, narrowly beating out United States Senator Orrin Hatch.

THE AFRICANIZED HONEYBEE

Long feared and unfairly shunned, in 1978 the LDS Church accepted Africanized honeybees, who were members in good standing, on an equal footing with their honeybee brethren.

JACKALOPE

Irrefutable proof that this member of the bunny family exists— and in large numbers— can be found on postcard racks throughout the West.

JACKASSALOPE

A resident of the 400,000 square-mile would-be-wilderness, this mulish defender of pristine habitat is actively despised and reviled by Utah legislators. Considered by developers and off-road vehicle proponents to be a vermin with litigious tendencies, the jackassalope is nonetheless revered by many Utahns for its stubborn refusal to give an inch.

ROADKILL

Statistics indicate an alarming increase in roadkill.

Researchers at the University of Utah have charted a convincing connection between miles of paved roads and roadkill. Projecting into the future, at current rates, we will soon be up to our armpits in roadkill.

To forestall roadkill propagation and the nightmare of being swamped in a roadkill tsunami, experts recommend a decrease in the miles of paved roads.

DEER MOUSE

*Killer Without
a Conscience*

The Deer Mouse has killed more Utahns than have bears, wolves and mountain lions combined. In fact, the latter three are responsible for a total of one fatality in the last hundred and sixty years of white settlement.

It may look innocent, but this clever rodent isn't above using biological warfare against humanity.

In 1993 a Hanta virus outbreak in the Four Corners area killed 50% of those who contracted the disease, which in its early stages mimics the flu. The disease was traced back to deer mouse droppings.

Homeland Security is looking to connect the mouse and a surreptitious meeting with an Al Qaeda operative in Budapest in 1992.

FLORA

Flora is your good-hearted neighbor who is there with a smile, a plate of cookies and a bucket of empathy when you need it.

Utah is lousy with this species. Thank God.

DESSERT in the DESERET DESERT

Utah Cuisine

DESERET DINING

Think "filling."

Typical Utah fare goes back to the pioneers. Stalked by the constant spectre of crop failure, drought, blight and starvation, Utahns learned to pack it away before the rats and crickets got to it.

Eating whatever happens to be at hand has led to some interesting culinary treats.

Take funeral potatoes—a casserole made with lots of starch (potatoes) and fat (cheese, butter/margarine), and generously sprinkled on top with crushed potato chips (more starch and fat).

"MY PRECIOUS!"

MORMON MUFFIN RECIPE

Utah cuisine consists of dishes designed to feed, if not multitudes, then a good portion of the neighborhood. And the neighborhood is happy to eat it up. Mormon cookery uses commonplace ingredients to produce uncommon results. Mormon Muffins are a good example.

2 cups boiling water	5 cups flour
5 tsp. baking soda	1 tsp. salt
1 cup shortening	4 cups all-bran cereal
2 cups sugar	2 cups bran flakes
4 eggs	1 cup walnuts
1 qt. buttermilk	(chopped)

DIRECTIONS: Stir soda into boiling water. Set aside.

Whip shortening and sugar together, then beat eggs slowly into mixture, one at a time. Add buttermilk, flour and salt. Mix well. Slowly add soda water. Fold cereal and walnuts into mixture.

Leave muffin mix in refrigerator overnight (optional).

Fill greased muffin tins about 1/2 full. Bake in pre-heated oven at 350°F for 25 to 30 minutes. Let cool. Makes about 4 dozen.

JELL-O™

Green Jell-O™
is celebrated
as *the* Utah
foodstuff—no
one knows why,
as it contains no
starch or fat.

No one eats more of the gelatin dessert per
capita than Utahns, except for a brief period
in the 80s when Iowa edged ahead. When
news broke that we were losing the great
Jell-O™ race, Utahns marched down to the
dessert aisle of their grocer and wrestled
back the jiggly gelatin crown.

THE GREEN JELL-O™ OLYMPIC PIN

Every Olympics features its own pins
inspired by a local theme.
In Utah, it was food. There were
soda pins, burger pins,
french fry pins. Yes, even
funeral potato pins.

*In the 2002 pin frenzy, which briefly
seized otherwise prudent Utah folk,
"Green Jell-O™" went for $300.*

The following resolution urging Jell-O™ recognition was passed in the 2001 General Session of the Utah Legislature. (This is not a joke).

SENATE RESOLUTION 0005

This Senate Resolution of the Legislature recognizes Jell-O™ brand gelatin as a favorite snack of Utah
Be it resolved by the Senate of the state of Utah:
WHEREAS, Utah has been the number one per capita consumer of Jell-O™ brand gelatin for many years;
WHEREAS, Jell-O™ is representative of good family fun, which Utah is known for throughout the world;
WHEREAS, Salt Lake Magazine proclaimed Utah "the Jell-O™ State" in a cover story in 1996;
WHEREAS, Jell-O™ brand gelatin recipes, which often include bananas, apples, marshmallow, pretzels, carrots and grapes, are a traditional favorite at family, church and community dinners throughout the Beehive State;
WHEREAS, in 1997, *Salt Lake Tribune* editorial cartoonist Pat Bagley drew a week-long series of political cartoons showcasing Jell-O™ in Utah in conjunction with the 100th anniversary of Jell-O™;
WHEREAS, a 2002 Winter Olympic pin was designed that featured a bowl of green gelatin and has become a valuable collector's item;
WHEREAS, when Des Moines, Iowa, edged out Salt Lake City as the capitol of Jell-O™ gelatin consumption in 1999, it sparked front page stories in Salt Lake City's newspapers;
WHEREAS, Utahns rallied to "Take Back the Title" as Chef Scott Blackerby hosted a recipe contest in the Hotel Monaco's Bambara Restaurant and Pat Bagley ran a cartoon persuading Utahns to purchase more Jell-O™ gelatin;
WHEREAS, throughout 2000, Brigham Young University students campaigned to make Utah's love of Jell-O™ official at festivals and fairs throughout Utah;
WHEREAS, more than 14,000 signatures have been collected from the people of Utah in support of the campaign to select Jell-O™ as the Official Snack of Utah; and
WHEREAS, due to these and many other efforts, Salt Lake City has now successfully recaptured the title:
NOW, THEREFORE, BE IT RESOLVED
that the Senate of the state of Utah recognize Jell-O™ as a favorite snack food of Utah.
BE IT FURTHER RESOLVED that a copy of this resolution be sent to Kraft Foods, Inc.

UTAHNICA

Deseret Data

UTAHNICS

How to talk Utahn

Some words that, despite all evidence to the contrary, are English:

Brothern — male fellow religionist

Crick — a small stream

Fark — an eating utensil

Ignernt — uneducated, lacking refinement

Jell — prison, slammer, pokey

Pell — pallid, as in, "You're looking pell.";
    also, bucket, container;
    also, medicine, pharmaceutical dose

Pellow — that thing you put your head on

Presheeyatcha — thanks

Shore — term of assent; response in the
    affirmative; as in, "Yes."

Sluff — to skip school

Speerchul — feeling of religiosity

Wuff — wild member of the canine family

UTAH SWEARING

"Oh my heck!" is an expression favored by Utahns; often employed to show surprise, delight or aggravation. It is what Utahns say instead of "@%$£¡¢!"

With Utah's strong religious morals, many consider swearing not only crude and offensive, but sinful as well.

Nonetheless, there are times when quiet reflection just won't do, even for the godly. Utahns have come up with substitutes to more fully express oneself in a kinda sorta forceful way.

darn

dang

flip

fetch

fudge

jeez

scrud

shoot

UTAH BY THE NUMBERS

State population: 2.5 million

Population of Salt Lake Valley in 1849: 8,000

Population of Salt Lake Valley today: 1.3 million

Median age in Utah: 26

Rank of Utah's population among the fifty states: 35th

Hispanic population: 200,000

Asian population: 40,000

Native American population: 30,000

African-American population: 20,000

Of every ten Utahns, number who are Mormon: 7

Polygamists incarcerated in the 1800s: 1,200

Number of people in the Mormon Tabernacle Choir: 325

Utah's highest point: King's Peak (13,528 feet)

Utah's lowest point: Beaverdam Creek (2,000 feet)

Depth of ancient Lake Bonneville: 1,000 feet

Average depth of the Great Salt Lake: 10 feet

Depth of the Kennecott copper mine: One-half mile

Cancer rate in Utah: half the national average

Record low temperature: -69° Fahrenheit

Record high temperature: 117 ° Fahrenheit

Square mileage: 85,000

Percentage of Utah that is forested: 28

Number of plant species in Utah: 4,000

Age of bristlecone pines in Bryce Canyon: 4,000 years

Number of stone arches in Arches National Park: 1,500

UTAH DESERADATA

State Symbol: The Beehive

State Hymn: "Utah We Love Thee"

State Humm: Buzzzzzzzz

State Hairstyle: The Beehive

State Bird: California Seagull

State Tree: Colorado Blue Spruce

State Slogan: "Utah: Gateway to Nevada"

State of Denial: Homosexuality is a choice

State Motto: The Behave State

State Fossil: *allosaurus fragilis*

State Dinosaur: Utah Legislator

State Church: Need you ask?

State Song: "Utah Uber Alles"

State Hamburger: Hires

State Drink: Diet Coke™ in a paper bag

State Drinking Song: "I Am a Utah Man, Sir!"